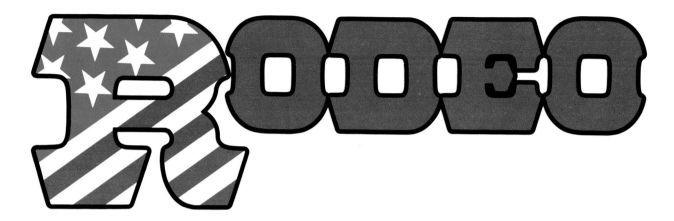

RODEO

Cheryl Walsh Bellville

Carolrhoda Books, Inc./Minneapolis

I would like to thank all the rodeo committees, stock contractors, and individuals who helped me get the pictures I needed for this book. Special thanks to Sally and Julie Dorweiler for their ideas.

Manufactured in the United States of America

This book is available in two editions:
Library binding by Carolrhoda Books, Inc.
Soft cover by First Avenue Editions
241 First Avenue North
Minneapolis, Minnesota 55401

LIBRARY OF CONGRESS CATALOGING IN PUBLICATION DATA

Bellville, Cheryl Walsh.
   Rodeo.

   Summary: Describes a rodeo and its component events such as bareback bronc riding, calf-roping, and steer wrestling.
   1. Rodeos—United States—Juvenile literature.
[1. Rodeos] I. Title.
GV1834.5.B45   1985   791′.8   84-14981
ISBN 0-87614-272-2 (lib. bdg.)
ISBN 0-87614-492-X (pbk.)

  5 6 7 8 9 10 98 97 96 95 94 93

For my sister Pam,
who has always been ready at the drop of a hat
to take off with me for a rodeo

Rodeo! The very sound of the word conjures up the Old West.

Our word rodeo comes from a Spanish word meaning roundup, and today's rodeo events originated from the skills cowboys needed during roundups or for general ranch work. Every ranch had broncos (untamed horses), and cowboys were forever bragging that they could ride anything with four legs! In the 1800s, cattle outfits sometimes challenged one another to bronc-riding contests, giving the cowboys a chance to prove their boasts.

7

8

There were no fenced-in arenas, chutes, or time limits in the old days. A cowboy simply got aboard a bronco and rode it until it stopped bucking, or until the horse won and the cowboy hit the dirt. This was pretty exciting sport, so about 100 years ago, in the territory that would one day become Arizona, someone decided to charge admission. The sport of rodeo was born.

Today there are rodeos throughout the United States, including Hawaii and Alaska, and in Canada. To that first rodeo event of bronc riding have been added roping, bull riding, steer wrestling, barrel racing, and many other events. Rodeo is no longer limited to ranch hands either. There are now rodeos for men and women, high school and college students, and "Little Britches" and 4-H rodeos for children.

People who ride rodeo are an independent sort. On the professional circuits there are no teams, no coaches, and few sponsors. The contestants are on their own and pay their own ways. Their attitude is often that they are competing against themselves— not against the contestants who rode before them, but against their own last rides. It's common to see one bull rider telling another everything the first knows about the bull the second is about to ride, actually helping another rider to win the competition.

Everyone in rodeo spends a lot of time on the road traveling from one rodeo to another. Bronc and bull riders can pick up and go with only a gear bag, but clowns and people who use their own horses in events (barrel racers, ropers, steer wrestlers, and others) must travel in vans, trailers, and campers.

Between traveling expenses, entry fees, and other costs, most people feel that if they win enough money to break even they are doing well, and some riders "buddy up" with others to share traveling expenses. Rodeo is not a profitable business, it's a choice of lifestyle.

Every rodeo begins with the Grand Entry. Contestants, local saddle clubs, members of the rodeo committee, clowns, and local officials all get into the act. The national flag is presented, the national anthem is sung, and the show is ready to begin.

The first event of the day is bareback bronc riding. Before the rodeo, the horses were drawn by number for each contestant by the rodeo judge. These stock numbers were posted so that the riders knew beforehand which horses they would be riding. The luck of the draw is very important to a cowboy's chances of winning because scores are based not only on the ride the cowboy makes but on the performance of the horse as well.

Animals are everything to rodeo, and good bucking horses are worth thousands of dollars. Some ranches raise bucking stock, hoping that an ornery mare will have an ornery foal. There are rodeo scouts who travel around the country following up rumors of horses that have "gone sour." There are even bucking horse auctions.

The life of a rodeo bronc isn't bad. Western artist and writer Sam Savitt once observed that a bronc might work only 10 seconds a week. The rest of the time he's standing around a corral eating and resting, and a good part of the year he's out to pasture doing nothing.

All a bareback rider has to hold onto during his wild ride is a rigging strapped around the horse just behind its withers (the top of its shoulders), and he can only hold on with one hand. If the rider's free hand touches the horse anywhere, he will be disqualified.

A rider must stay aboard for 8 seconds, and not just hanging on. The position of his spurs is watched from the very beginning of the ride when they must be up on the shoulder of the horse. If a rider spurs and rides with style and if the horse bucks well and if the rider lasts the 8 seconds, that's a good ride.

This rider had some problems with his ride, and now, to add insult to injury, he's being heckled by clown Quail Dobbs. Everyone is fair game for teasing from the clowns.

At the opposite end of the arena from the bucking chutes are the chutes used for timed events such as roping and steer wrestling. In these events the fastest time wins.

For the calf-roping event, the cowboy and his horse are in an open box with a rope barrier at one end. The calf is in an enclosed chute next to them. An experienced roping horse has every muscle tensed while it waits for the calf to be released. If in its excitement a horse breaks through the barrier before the calf has been released, a 10-second penalty is added to the roper's time. This almost certainly takes that roper out of the winnings.

The roper gives a nod to open the gate, and the calf takes off. As his horse positions itself alongside the calf, the roper gets his loop open. Any kind of catch is legal, but

the roper tries to drop his loop over the calf's head.

When the calf hits the end of the rope, the roper jumps from his horse and races to it. He picks the calf up by the flank, throws it down, and ties three of its legs together with a short rope called a piggin string. Then he throws his hands up to signal that he is done, and his time is recorded.

A good roping horse knows exactly what it is doing. As soon as the calf is flanked, it backs up just enough to keep the rope tight and prevent the calf from moving around. During the whole process the horse never takes its eyes off the calf.

Roping horses can make a lot of money for their owners and are treated with respect and affection. Some ropers even loan out their horses to other ropers for a percentage of the winnings.

Another roping event is team roping. In this event two ropers compete as a team to rope a steer. One roper puts a loop over the steer's head. That person is called the header. His partner aims for the steer's hind feet. That roper is called the heeler.

Roping originated during the days of the open range when there were no pens. If cattle needed attention, they were roped from horseback and worked on right out in the open. Both calf roping and team roping are skills that are still used today to manage cattle on ranches.

A saddle bronc doesn't just leave a chute, it explodes from it!

A saddle-bronc rider might seem to have an advantage over a bareback rider because of the rein and stirrups, but if the rider's foot comes out of the stirrup he is disquali-fied, and the rein is of no use at all in controlling the horse. The saddle has the horn removed so that the cowboy won't be hurt by ramming into it, and he couldn't use it even if it was there because this is strictly a one-handed event.

When the whistle blows the signal that the ride is over, pick-up men ride alongside the bronc. One of them grabs the rein, and the rider vaults over the back of the pick-up man's horse and onto the ground.

Some bucking horses are such professionals that they will buck for all they're worth until they hear the whistle and then simply quit.

There have always been women bronc riders and ropers, and in the old Wild West shows there were many female contestants. Somewhere along the line, though, someone decided that audiences didn't want to see women hurt in rough events like bronc riding, and they were limited to competition in barrel racing. Although women are again competing in other rodeo events, barrel racing remains important to most women and girls in rodeo.

Three barrels are set up in a cloverleaf pattern in the arena, two at one end and a third between them at the other end. Contestants may start from either of the first two barrels. They race around that barrel and take off for the second, make a reverse turn around the second and run for the third, round the third and race for the finish line.

The horses in this event run at top speed and an electronic timer is used to determine their times to 1/100 of a second. These horses usually come from race horse stock, and many have raced on a track. Most of them are trained for barrel racing by the women who ride them, and competition is fierce.

Steer wrestling, often called bull dogging, is a timed event in which the steer wrestler, called a dogger, jumps from a running horse onto a running steer and wrestles the steer to the ground. Another rider, called a hazer, rides on the other side of the steer and tries to keep it in position for the dogger.

This event is not just a matter of strength. It takes balance and timing to be in just the right position to bring down the steer, and the show can get pretty exciting. More than one steer has turned and crossed paths with a running horse, causing some spectacular crashes.

The order of events at different rodeos may vary, but one event is always saved for last: bull riding. This wild and dangerous event is a real crowd pleaser.

The bull rider uses a flat, braided rope to ride the bull. The rope is wrapped around the bull and around the rider's hand and is not tied in any way. The rules say it must be a loose rope. A bell hanging beneath the bull weights the rope so that it will fall off after the ride and also warns everyone in the arena that a bull is out.

Bull riding is a one-handed ride, but there are no other rules. A bull rider just does his darnedest to stay on. One cowboy said it wasn't the bull riding that worried him, it was the getting off! Even when the rider is still aboard, a clown sticks pretty close to the bull so he'll be right there to help out if he's needed.

Clown Ronn Taylor is also a talented bullfighter.

Rodeo clowns are somewhat misnamed today. In early rodeos a clown's main job was to make jokes and entertain the crowd. Today's rodeo clowns are still very funny, but their main job is to protect the bull riders. When a bull rider is in trouble, the clown draws the bull's attention to himself, giving the cowboy time to run for safety.

Rodeo people call the clowns barrel men and bullfighters. The clowns often work in pairs during the bull riding. One of them, the barrel man, will be inside a barrel taunting the bull. When the bull comes at the barrel, the barrel man ducks inside. The other clown, the bullfighter, will sometimes run in circles around the bull and even jump over the bull's head!

Outrunning a bull is no easy feat, and in mud like this it's even more treacherous. Wick Peth is one clown who can manage in any situation. In the barrel is Tom Feller.

Rodeo takes many forms today. There are small, local rodeos and world-championship rodeos. Some rodeos have additional events such as goat tying, ribbon roping, or pole bending. Between events you may see anything from trick riding to trained buffalo to border collies herding ducks. The number of rodeos and the people involved with them grows every year, assuring a future for the sport and keeping this chapter of the saga of the Old West alive for us all.